YUIMA NAKAZATO

Behind the Design

YUIMA NAKAZATO

Behind the Design

服の、先へ

Book design and layout by Ai Yoshino.
Published in 2022 by Bookend Co., Ltd., Tokyo
Printed in Japan by Nissha Printing Communications, Inc.
ISBN 978-4-907083-76-2

Golden Record Inspiration

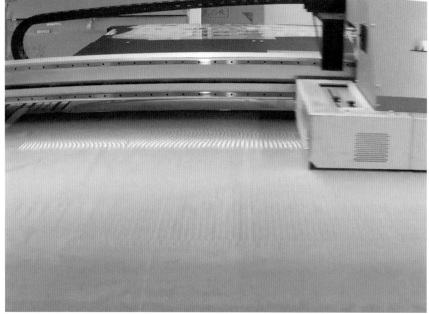

Biosmocking

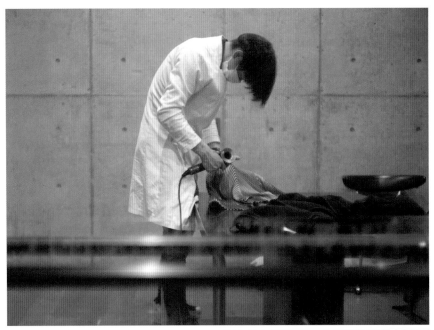

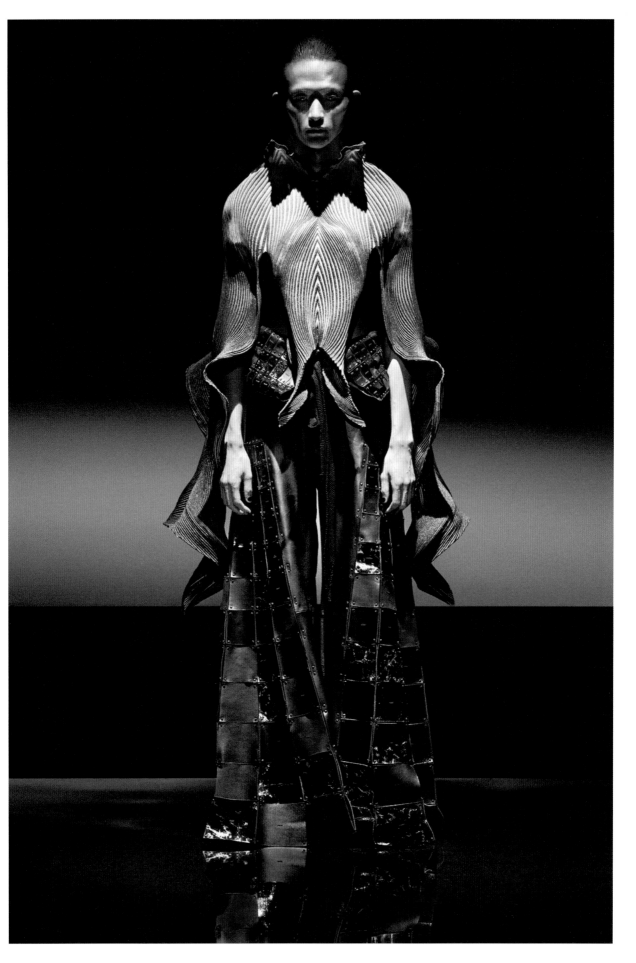

Sound Visualization

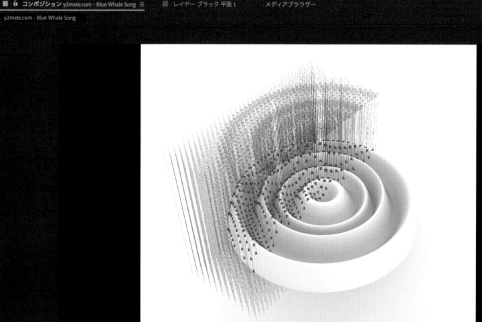

100 %   ∨   (フル画質)   ∨   🔄 🔳 🔲 🔳 🔳   🔦 🔅 +0.0   📷   0;00;00;00

ユー

🖉 🔳   🎦 🏛 🗐 🖉 🗀   親とリンク   00s   02s   04s   06s   08s   10s   12s   14s   16s   18s   20s   22s   24s   26s

∖ fx 🔳 🖉 🔮 🖸   🕼 なし   ∨

∕ fx 🔳 🔮 🖸   🕼 なし   ∨

∕ fx 🔳 🔮 🖸   🕼 なし   ∨

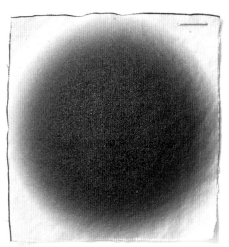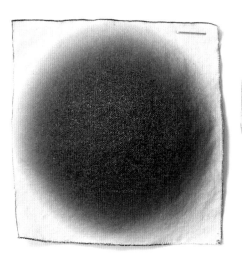

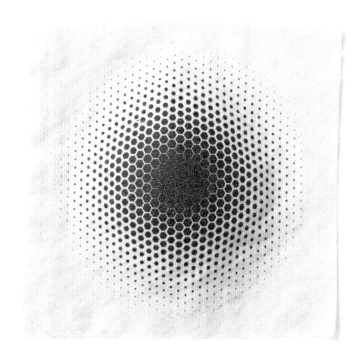

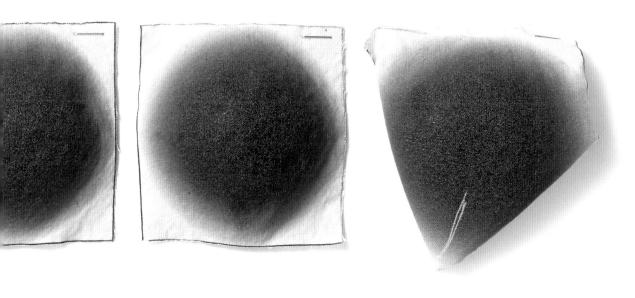

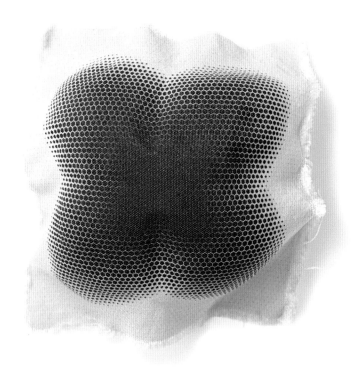

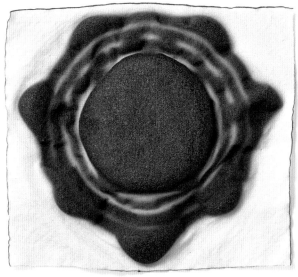

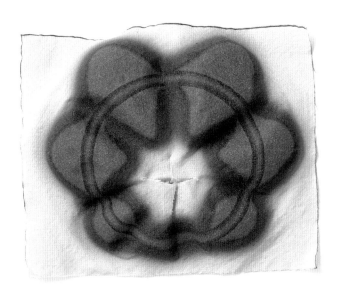

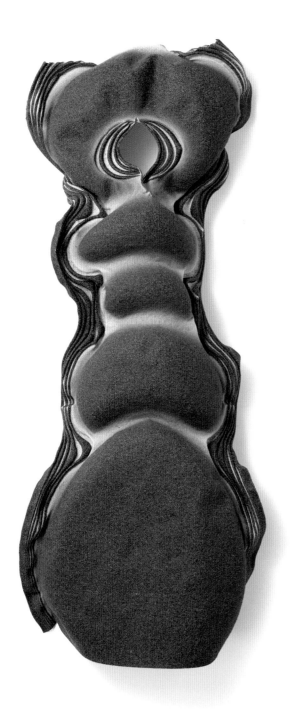
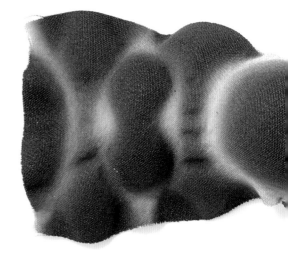

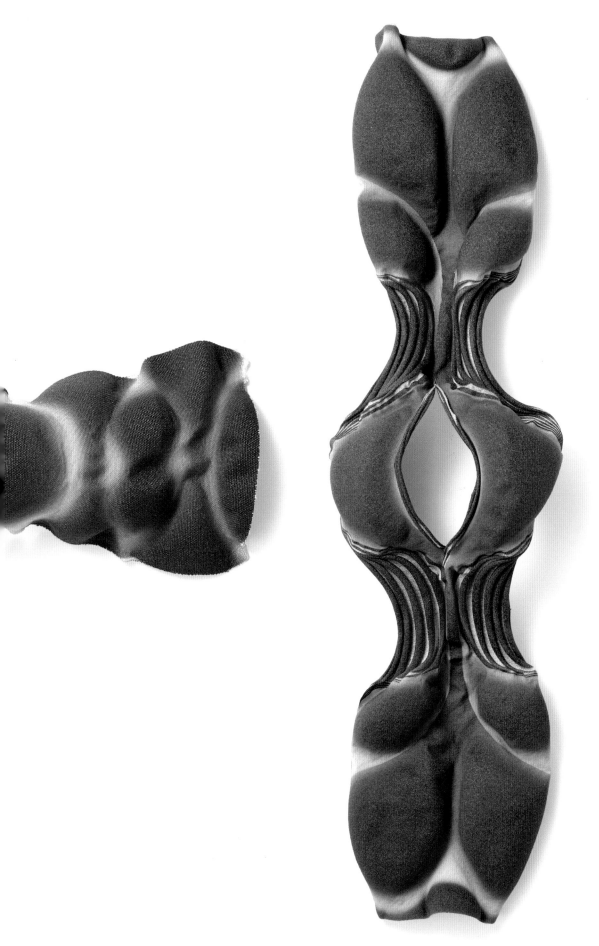

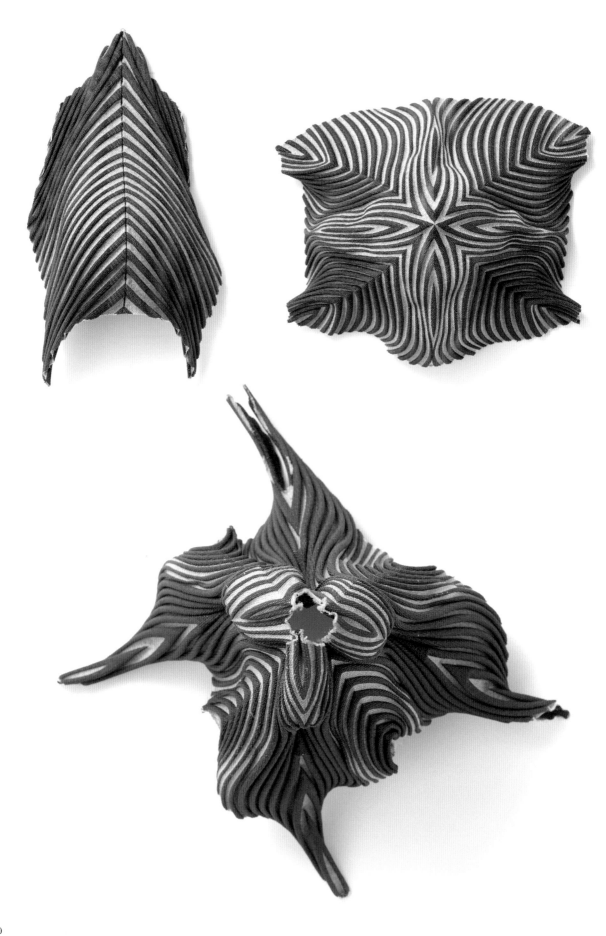

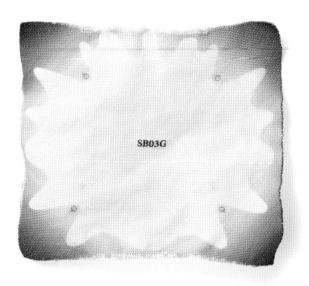

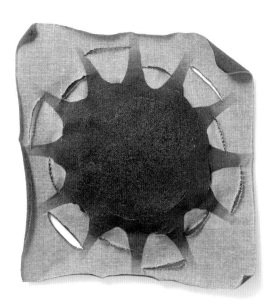

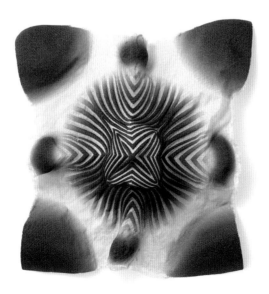

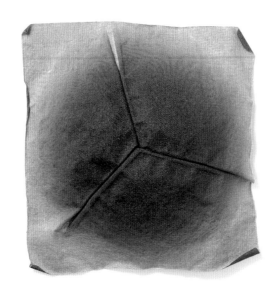

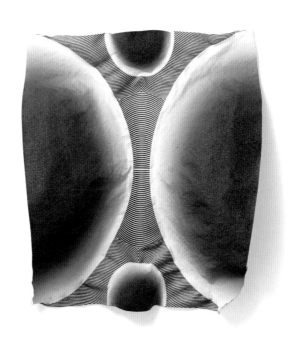

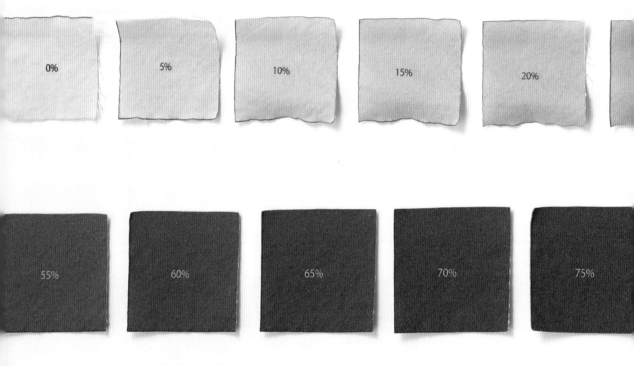

Technological Evolution

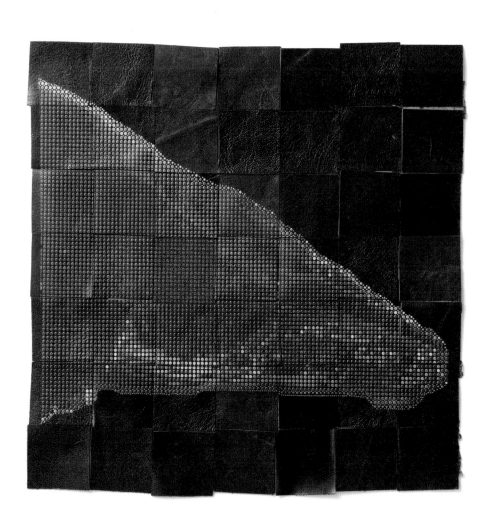

KNIT JACKET

BACK

FRONT

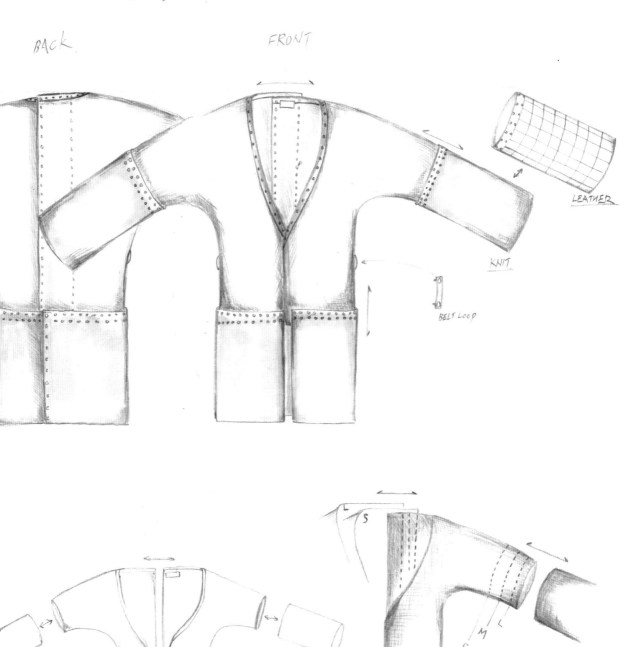

LEATHER

KNIT

BELT LOOP

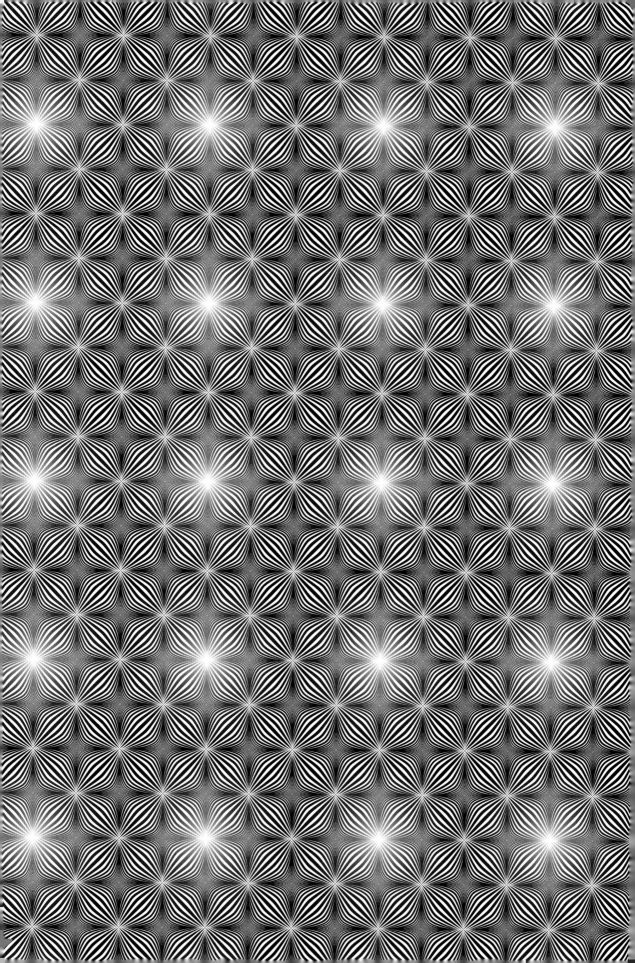

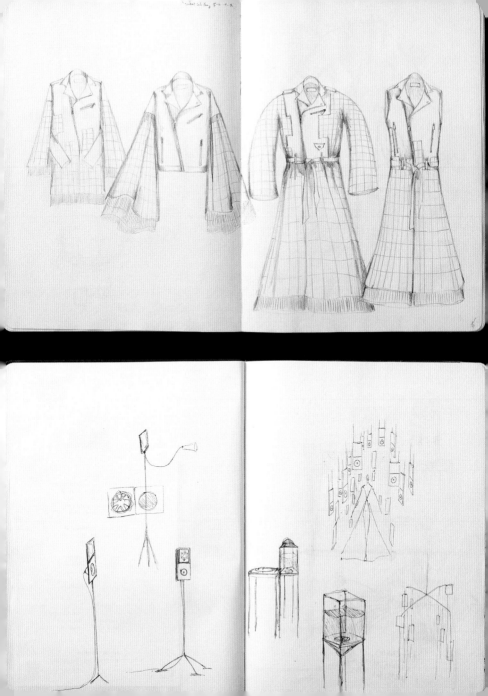

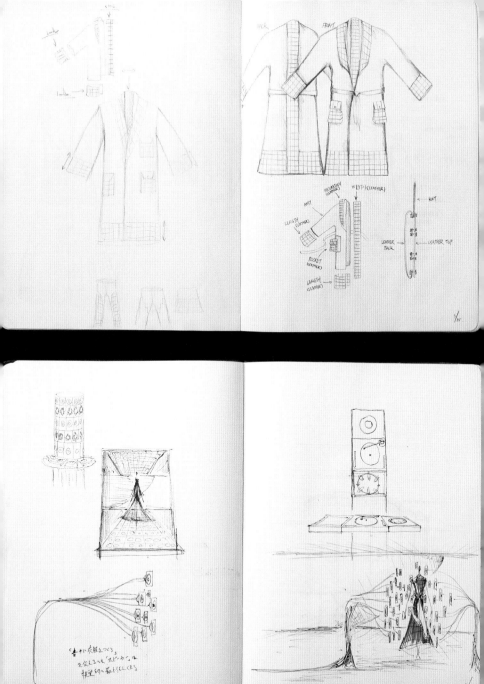

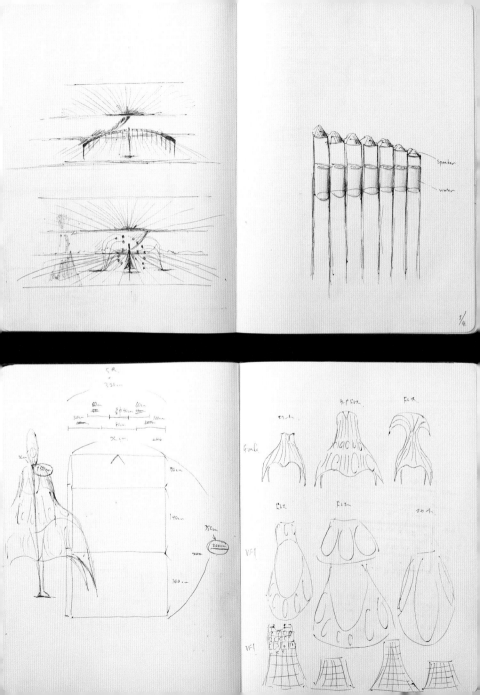

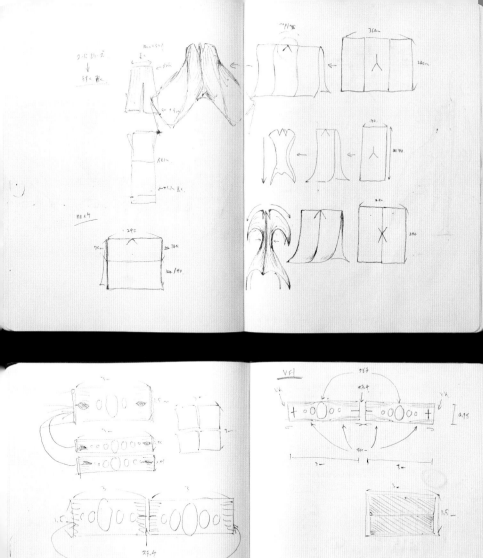

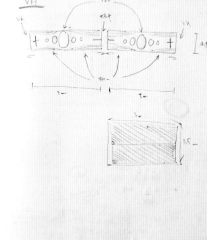

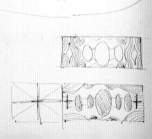

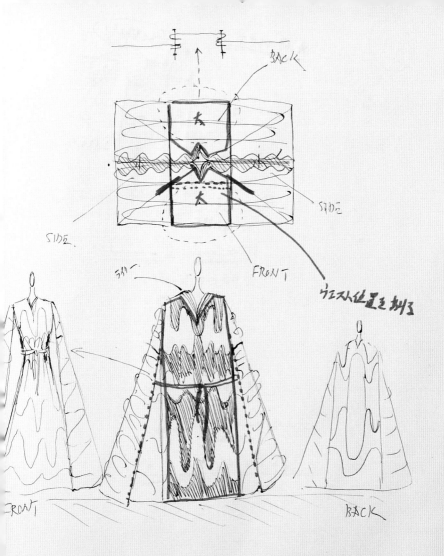

BACK

SIDE

SIDE

FRONT

ウエスト位置を上げる

FRONT

BACK

Runway Show

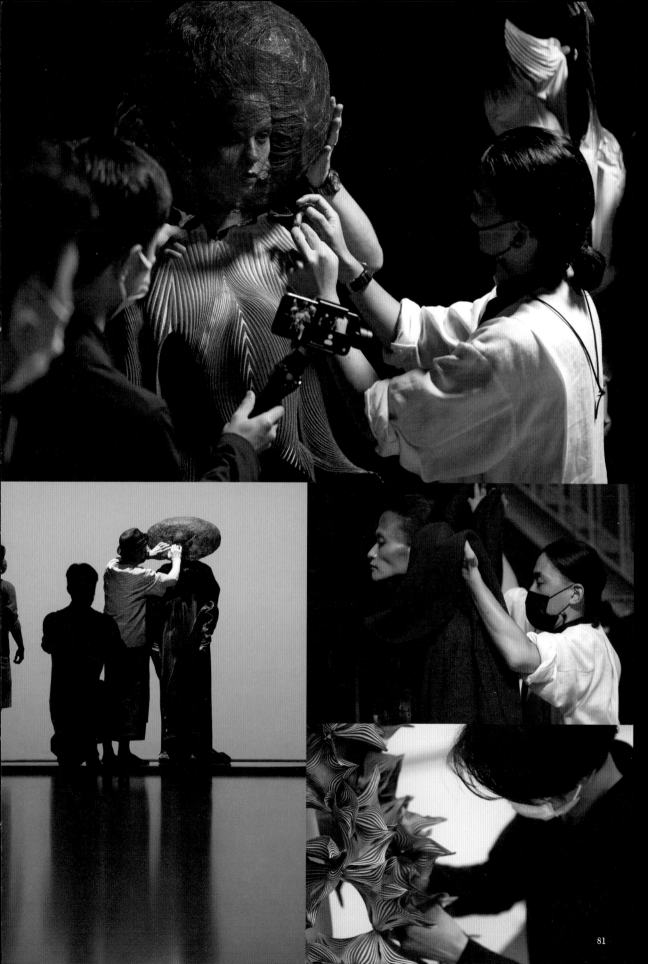

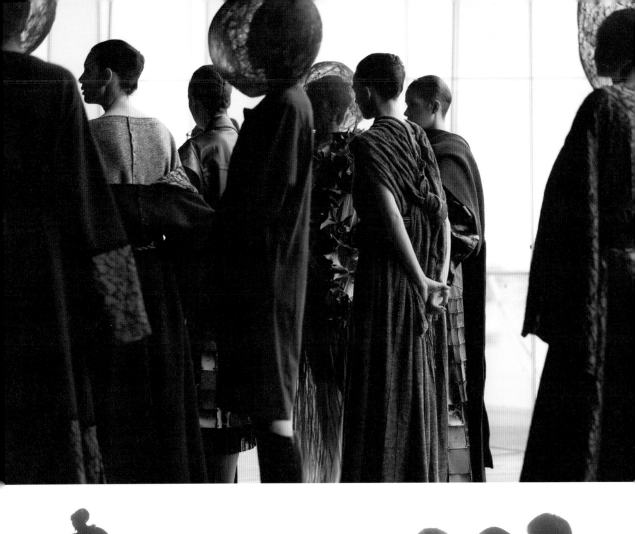

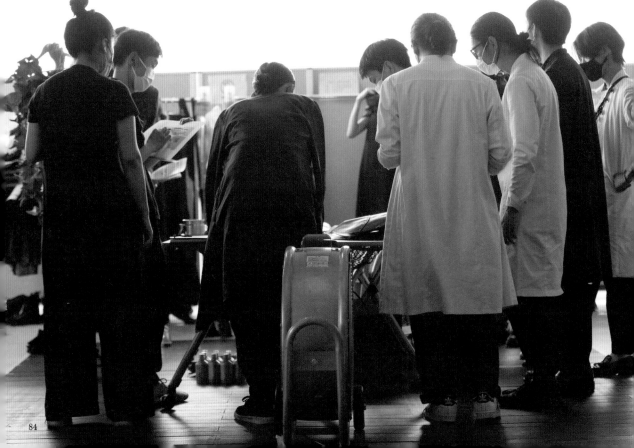

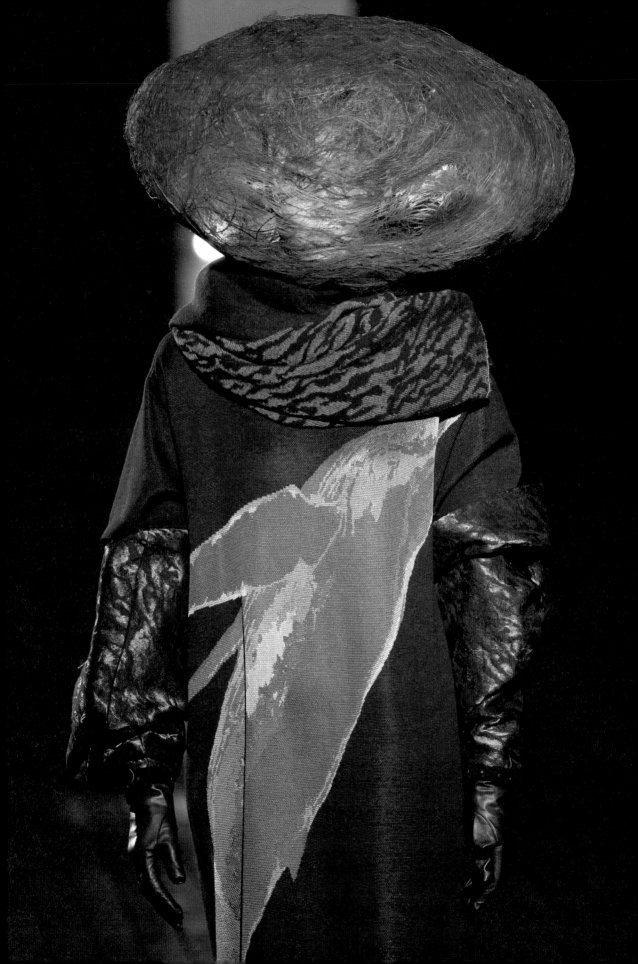

Yuima Nakazato Collections:
2019-2022

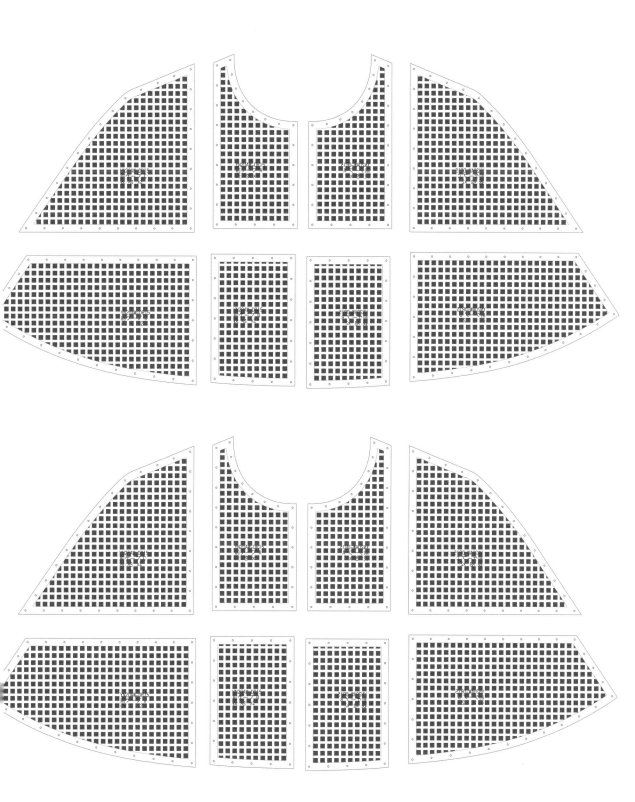

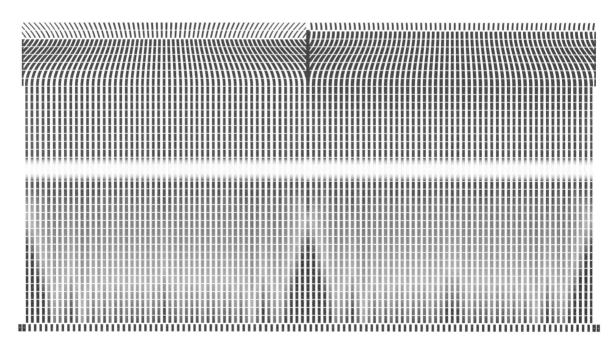

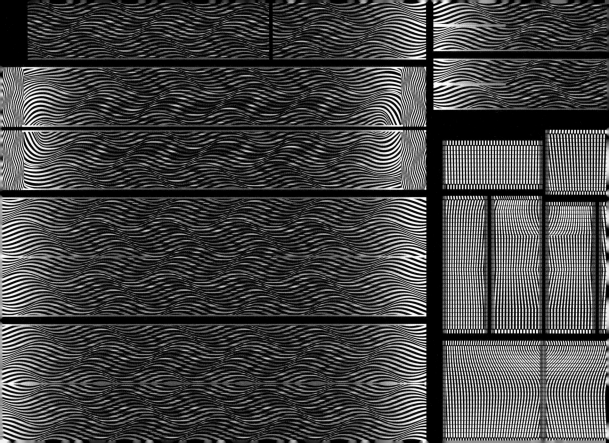

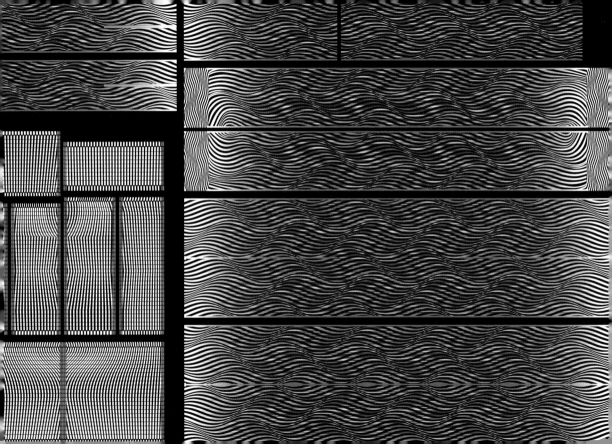

「EVOKE」が生まれた思想の背景、衣服になるまでのプロセス、
そして「服の、先へ」どんなヴィジョンを描いていたか。

1 ――― 音との出会い

　2021年2月に「ATLAS」の発表を終え、すぐに新しいコレクションの制作に
入ったのですが、コロナ禍により、過去2回のコレクションは映像をデジタルで
配信する形式が続き、先の見通しも立たず、閉塞感を抱えていました。
　しかし、その一方で、パンデミックで時代が大きく変わっていくのではないか
という希望もうっすら感じるようになっていました。「新しい時代」のデザインにつ
いて考えているうちに、ふと頭に浮かんだのが、「音」でした。
　コロナ禍で移動が制限され、ほとんどの情報をインターネットから得るように
なると、どうしても視覚情報が優位性をもってしまう。その状況に飽き足らず、
もっと刺激を与えてくれるインフォーメーションを探し求めていると、音の世界に
なんとなく心地よさを感じたり、人の声を聞いていると安心感を覚えるようにな
りました。それが「ATLAS」の発表直後のことで、音の世界からコレクションを
組み立ててみようと考えたのが、最初の一歩です。
　人の声は、骨格などの身体情報や、話すスピード、抑揚や感情表現からく
る音の高低など、いろいろな要素から生まれるもので、その人の"人となり"が
声に現れています。つまり、その人の"アイデンティティ"とも言える声を、衣服の
デザインに表現することができたなら、それは究極の一点物として、新しいオー
トクチュールの扉を開くきっかけになるのではないか。そう考えたわけです。

2 ――― シンボルとしてのクジラ

　「音」や「声」についてリサーチを進めていくなかで、たまたま22.2チャンネル
というNHKのスーパーハイビジョン（8K）で使われている超高性能サラウンドで
音を聞く機会がありました。室内をぐるりと囲むように設置された22個のスピー
カーとサブウーファー2個から音が流れてくる空間で目を閉じてその音を聞いて
いると、音に形とか物質のような重さを感じるようになりました。音から形を感じ
るということは、音を「見ている」のではないか――見ているのか、感じている
のか、聞いているのか、よくわからない非常に不思議な体験でした。
　この経験によって、音から何か形のようなものを作り出すことができるのではな
いかと考えたのです。音という形のないものから形を掘り起こしていくことに、
デザインの新しい可能性を感じて、試行錯誤を始めていきました。
　音についてさらに調べていくなかで、1977年にNASAが打ち上げた探査機ボ
イジャーに搭載されたレコード盤に関する情報に出会いました。これは「ゴール

fig. 1

デンレコード」と呼ばれ、地球の生命や文化を伝える様々な音や画像を収録し、地球外生命体や未来の人類が見つけて解読することを目的として作られたものです。ゴールデンレコードに収録された様々な音声のなかに、人間の声とクジラの声を重ね合わせたセクションがあり、そのユニークな視点に興味が湧きました。クジラの鳴き声は非常に美しく、また何かを伝えようと、コミュニケーションをとっていることが伝わってきます。（➡︎ pp.18-19）

ボイジャーが打ち上げられた1970年代は、クジラが環境問題や生命体としての地球のメタファとして認知され始めた時期です。それから半世紀を経て、今度は新しい時代への変わり目、希望のシンボルとして、今回のコレクションに使ってみたいという気持ちが湧きました。こうして、クジラの鳴き声がインスピレーションとなって、「EVOKE」というコンセプトが決まりました。

3——— 一枚の長方形の布から衣服を生成する技術

もう一つの大事な要素として、EVOKE がパリでの10回目のコレクションになったことです。2016年からパリでコレクションを発表するようになって、毎シーズン発表し続けるなかで、独自の進化を遂げてきたと思います。

例えば、「TYPE-1」というシステムには、その前段階として小さなパーツが寄り集まって一着の服ができあがる「ユニット・コンストラクティッド・テキスタイル」という技法がありました。技術の進化とともにコレクションも発展してきており、そしてそれが、今の「Biosmocking[☆1]」という新しい技術にもつながっています（figs.1, 2）。

☆1——— Biosmocking は構造タンパク質の Brewed Protein™ 素材を使って、同素材でしかできない生地の立体成形技術のこと

これまで培ってきた技術やアイデアを点とすると、その点をすべてつなぎ合わせて一つに収斂させる、それが EVOKE でやりたかったことであり、10回目という節目での集大成としての目的でもありました。

このように「まとめ」を意識しながら、クジラのインスピレーションを膨らませ、まずデザイン画に落とし込んでいきました（figs. 5, p. 134）。クジラのモチーフが服の上を泳いでいるダイレクトなものもあれば、クジラの柄を絵羽模様にあしらった訪問着のようなドレスもあります。（➡︎ pp.21-23）着物のように一枚の長方形の布から衣服の形を生成する技法はこれまでも採り入れてきました。（➡︎ pp.117, 120, 126-27）これを EVOKE では Biosmocking という新しい技術で継続しています。（➡︎ pp.63, 65）

4——— Biosmocking のプロセス

まず、デザイン画をもとに、Biosmocking のデータを作り、布に印刷します。その布を70度のお湯に1分間浸すと布が水を吸い込んで縮み、さらに布の水分を飛ばして乾燥させると、一着のドレスができあがります。（➡︎ pp.24-27）

つまり、布に印刷された柄によって部分的に伸縮が起こり、平面だった布が三次元の凹凸のある身体にピタリと沿う立体に変化するわけです。これは、植物由来の糖類を原料に、微生物による発酵で作られる構造タンパク質「ブリュード・プロテイン素材」がもつ「スーパーコントラクション」という縮む性質を、デジ

fig. 2

タル技術を使ってコントロールすることによって、立体的な形状が生まれるという技術です。この全く新しい衣服の生成技術を「Biosmocking」と呼んでいます。

　ATLASで初めて採用したこのBiosmockingを、EVOKEでは音声を視覚化したデータを使って衣服を作ることができないかと考え、実験を始めました。

　実験では、まずガラスの器に食品用のラップフィルムを貼り、その上に塩の粒を並べて大きな音を発するとフィルムが振動し、その衝撃で白い粒が動いて柄が生まれます。(→ p.29) これに着想を得て、まずはデジタル上で音を可視化するための仕組み作りを開始しました。同時に音を視覚化して立体を作るため、何回も小さな布片で実験を繰り返し、試行錯誤を重ねました。(→ pp.30-35, 38-40, 42, 44-46, 48-49)

5———— 究極の一点物

　実験を経て、ようやく音から立体を生み出すことに成功すると、今度はクジラの鳴き声をBiosmockingのデータに置き換え、そのデータを前述のように、布に印刷し、お湯に浸して乾燥させるプロセスを経て、ドレスができあがりました。不思議な凹凸や色彩、フォルムから成るこのドレスは、クジラの鳴き声が素材となって生成されたものです。

　もちろん人間の声であっても同じことが可能ですから、誰かの声を録音して、同じプロセスを繰り返せば、衣服ができあがります。その人のだけの服を作ることがオートクチュールの真髄であるとすれば、アイデンティティである「声」から生まれた衣服は、究極の一点物になります。これは新しいオートクチュールの扉を開くのではないかと考えました。

6———— スタイリストとの協働

　コレクションにおいて、次に重要な要素がスタイリングです。EVOKEでは、浮世絵に描かれた装束にインスピレーションを得て、帯の結び、重ね着、肩をちょっと落とした着方など、着物の様々な着こなしからインスピレーションを得ています。

　そしてEVOKEのスタイリングを完成させる上で重要な役割を担ったのがロンドン在住のスタイリスト、ロビー・スペンサー（Robbie Spencer）です。実は10年前に東京で初めてコレクションを発表した時に、彼がその作品 (fig. 3) をある雑誌で取り上げてくれて、私が表現したかった世界観を理解し、さらに昇華させてスタイリングしてくれたことが非常に印象的で、EVOKEでのコラボレーションを彼にオファーしたのです。

　ロビーの快諾を受け、彼の住むロンドンと、我々の東京のアトリエをリモートでつなぎ、前述の浮世絵の着こなしをどうすれば表現できるかを、スケッチや写真などの膨大な資料を共有し (figs. 7, p. 136)、議論や試行錯誤を重ねながら、一つのスタイリングに落とし込んでいきました。リモートによる作業は、とても挑戦的な試みだったのではないかと思います。

fig. 3

点字

レザーのコートドレスの上に、小さなドットでクジラの柄を描くアイデアは、点字からインスピレーションを得たもので、手で触ることでクジラの柄を「感じる」、「わかる」ような、エッジを効かせたデザインです (figs. 6, p.135)。そこには、触覚で衣服を感じることができるのではないかという挑戦も込められています。(⇒ p.53)

西陣織＋ブリュード・プロテイン™素材

日本の西陣織にブリュード・プロテイン繊維を組み込んで織った布を使ったドレスです。海の波をイメージした柄は、青く独特の光り方がBPによって生み出されています (fig. 4)。シルクとも化学繊維とも異なる高透明感と、発光のような不思議な光沢が特徴で、日本の伝統的な織物と最先端の技術が組み合わさった、新しいテキスタイルが生まれたのではないかと思います。(⇒ p.59)

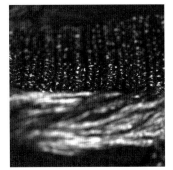

fig. 4

TYPE-1

針と糸を使わない技術「TYPE-1」の進化を表すウールのコートは、背中心で身幅を変化させ、サイズを変えることができます。この技術によって、いろいろな人の身体にフィットさせることができたり、袖と裾のパーツを取り替えれば、丈を長くしたり短くしたり (figs. 8, p.137)、デザインも変えられる。従来の「TYPE-1」より選択肢の自由度が増したことが進化といえます。(⇒ pp.60-61)

Biosmocking

長方形のパターンの中に、複雑に曲線が描かれていますが、中央の黒い十字が首を出す部分です。この十字に切り込みを入れ、布をお湯に浸して縮めると、傘が閉じるような形——十字の部分が上にせり上がるように膨らみ、周囲の部分が下がった立体——が生まれます。通常衣服を作る場合、前身頃と後身頃の2枚の布を組み合わせて身体を包み込んでいくのが基本ですが、それとはまったく違う次元の立体の生成方法によって、布をいっさい切り落とさずに、ここまで複雑な立体を作り出すことができます。また、デジタルデータのプリントによって形状をコントロールする技術のため、比較的容易に一人ひとりの身体や趣向に寄り添った衣服を考えることも可能です。

　小さなピースがつながり一つのドレスが生まれていくというアイデアは、2016年に初めてパリでコレクションを発表したときからのもので、当初は折り紙のように手作業で折りたたみながらピースを作っていました。EVOKEではこの発想をBiosmockingの技術を使って、ピースを分断せずに、1枚の布にパターンを展開することで、ピースをつなげたような複雑な立体の服を作りあげています。(⇒ p.65)

　EVOKE 以前の2シーズンは、デジタル映像をインターネットで配信する発表が続いていました。そこで、オンラインであっても、映像は従来のように人がシンプルに歩く姿を映像で伝えたいと考えました。

　会場は、横浜の大さん橋ホールという2,000㎡の非常に広い場所を、照明と演出を極限まで追求したものの、そのまま使っています。その会場をモデルが服を着てただ歩くのですが、もちろんモデルの歩き方や表情で服の力強さを伝えていくことは心がけました。ショーのなかで、モデルが一人ずつ出ていく場面は、かなり暗く、ダークな印象のある世界観ですが、後半では、舞台奥のカーテンが開いて、自然光が外から差し込んできます。暗闇の中から次の時代の希望を感じるようなイメージと、深海と海面を行き来しながら生きているクジラが、暗闇と光という二つの世界をつなぐ存在であるということを表現したものです。

　カーテンが開くタイミングを日没に合わせたのですが、開演ギリギリまで雨の予報だったので、よくても曇り空という気象条件でした。ところが、雨が上がり、カーテンが開くと外には奇跡のように夕焼けが広がっていたのです。広い会場の暗闇と外の明るい世界が混ざり合い、感動的な自然の演出が実現しました。さらに、ショーでは坂本龍一さんの曲に、クジラの鳴き声を重ね合わせ、音と光がすべてひとつに融合したかたちでフィナーレをむかえることができました。(⇒ pp.72-112)

　今はデジタル技術で映像にどんな加工もできてしまう時代ですが、今回は従来のランウェイにできる限り近いかたちで、ショーのライブの緊張感や、その生々しさのようなものも含めて映像から伝わる演出になっています。

How the Collection Took Shape
In the words of the designer

Yuima Nakazato describes the thinking that went into his Evoke—fall/winter 2021—collection; the process that culminated in the creation of the garments; and the positioning of fashion in his worldview.

1. Aural Encounters

Launching my Atlas—spring/summer 2021—collection in February 2021 meant getting started on the upcoming fall/winter collection. Covid-19 had obliged us to present our fall/winter 2020 and spring/summer 2021 collections online. I was resigned to remaining online with the next collection, but I perceived a gleam of hope. The pandemic was transforming the world in diverse ways, and that presented something of a basis for optimism. As I contemplated approaches to design for the new era, I hit on the notion of sound.

Covid-19 had restricted our freedom of movement and heightened our reliance on the Internet for information, predominantly through the visual vehicles of text and images. Frustration with that predominance steered me toward sound as a more stimulating medium. Listening to human voices was reassuring. Seeking that reassurance was the first step in conceiving what became the Evoke collection.

Our voice is a crystallization of our identity. Its timbre conveys information about our physique. Our personality unfolds in the speed at which we talk and in the contours of our verbal inflection.

A garment unique to its owner is the essence of haute couture. If we could transform a person's voice into a garment, that would be, I reasoned, haute couture's ultimate fulfillment. It would open the door to new possibilities in fashion.

2. Whale Songs

The opportunity arose while I was studying sound and voices to experience sound on a new plane. My experience was courtesy of ultrahigh-performance surround sound. Japan's public broadcaster, Nippon Hoso Kyokai (NHK), had developed the sound system for its 8K (about 8,000 pixels wide) Super Hi-Vision high-definition TV format. The system produces stunning audio effects through an array of 22 speakers and 2 subwoofers. Closing my eyes, I sensed a tangible substance in the sound that flowed through the room.

Sensing physical form in sound is akin to perceiving the sonic phenomena visually. And my encounter with NHK's 22.2-channel system awakened me to the potential for making something tangible from sound. Summoning form from the formless realm of sound promised to unleash new potential in design, and I set to work on the endeavor.

My work led me to audio data that the US National Aeronautics and Space Administration (NASA) launched into space in 1977. The data was on a gold-plated phonograph record that NASA loaded into each of the space probes Voyager 1 and 2. It encompassed numerous representations of earthborn life and culture, including a diversity of musical selections; a polyglot of spoken greetings; and a broad range of animal sounds, including the songs of humpback whales. The so-called Golden Record was a message to any extraterrestrial intelligent life that might happen upon either of the Voyagers. I found the endeavor

fig. 5

enchanting. The whale songs, especially, are extremely beautiful and convey a compelling sense of communicating something (⇢ pp. 18–19).

Whales had become a symbol of the fragility of the earthly ecosystem when NASA launched the Voyager probes in 1977. More than four decades later, we are entering a new phase of existence on this planet. Whales struck me as a potent symbol of human hopes and aspirations in the changing world, and their songs became the inspiration for the Evoke collection.

3. A Single Sheet of Fabric

Evoke would be the 10th collection that I had presented in Paris since my debut there in 2016, and each collection had marked a step in my evolution as a designer. That evolution has included advances in the technology that I use to create garments and in my design aesthetic.

One notable advance was the Type-1 system. The Type-1 technology started out as something that I dubbed "unit-constructed textiles." It was a methodology for combining multiple small parts into a single garment. Type-1 evolved into my Biosmocking methodology, which provides for crafting a garment from a single sheet of fabric, rather than from parts. What makes the Biosmocking process possible is the brewed protein, a product of microorganisms, that I employ for the fabric (Figs. 1, 2, p. 130).

All the advances that I had achieved in technology and all my aesthetic insights to date went into the Evoke collection. Linking everything was the inspiration that I had derived from whale songs. That inspiration was visible in literally rendered whale motifs seen swimming on some of the garments and in abstract renderings of whale imagery in kimono-like embellishment on others (⇢ pp. 21–23).

A kimono takes shape from a single rectangular sheet of fabric, and Biosmocking generates haute couture garments in the same manner (⇢ pp. 117, 120, 126–127). Biosmocking was the progenitive dynamic of the Evoke collection (⇢ pp. 63, 65).

4. Biosmocking

The Biosmocking process begins with digitizing the design drawings and imprinting them on fabric. We then submerge the fabric in warm, 70-degree-centigrade water for one minute. The fabric shrinks on absorbing water. Dried, it becomes a new dress (⇢ pp. 24–27).

What started out as a flat sheet of fabric has acquired a bumpy, three-dimensional configuration and has expanded and contracted in accordance with the imprinted design data. It has become a garment that fits snugly around the wearer. Biosmocking technology thus permits us to control the supercontractive behavior of the Brewed Protein™ fabrics and to generate three-dimensional garments in accordance with digitized designs.

We used Biosmocking for the first time in my Atlas—spring/summer 2021—collection. In preparing the Evoke collection, we began experimenting with an eye to visualizing sound in garments. We settled on an experimental methodology where we stretched vinyl food wrap over the upward-facing mouth of a glass vessel, sprinkled granules of salt on the wrap, and used highly amplified sound to vibrate the film and cause the granules to assume a pattern (⇢ p. 29).

Our experimentation illuminated the potential for visualizing sound and prompted us to tackle the visualization digitally. That was a precursor to translating the sound into three-dimensional forms. We achieved that translation through the trial and error of repeated experiments on small pieces of fabric (⇢ pp. 30–35, 38–40, 42, 44–46, 48–49).

fig. 6

5. One-of-a-Kind Creations

Having succeeded in translating sound into three-dimensional forms, we turned our attention to copying whale songs into the Biosmocking data. Then we created dresses through the process that I have described: imprinting the fabric with data, submerging it in warm water, and drying the garments-to-be. The resultant dresses, including their curious forms and textures, are tangible manifestations of the intangible sounds of whale songs.

What we did in creating dresses with whale songs we could also do with human voices. We were on track to achieve the fulfillment of haute couture that I had envisioned through sound.

6. The Stylist

A crucial factor in any collection is the stylist. In the Evoke collection, I drew inspiration from the kimono-clad figures in ukiyo-e woodblock prints. We incorporated obi sashes, multilayer frocks, and lowered shoulders. Putting the finishing touches on the presentation was the London-based stylist Robbie Spencer.

I had met Robbie 10 years earlier, when I presented my first collection in Tokyo. He introduced some of my works in a magazine article and displayed a good understanding of the worldview that I was attempting to convey. The way Robbie's styling carried my works to a higher plane had stayed with me, and it prompted me to turn to him for help with the Evoke collection (Fig. 3, p. 131).

Robbie graciously agreed to my request, whereupon we engaged in repeated virtual conferences between his London workplace and our Tokyo studio. He furnished all sorts of ideas for making the most of the ukiyo-e look. We exchanged countless sketches and photographs (Fig. 7), discussed matters from every angle, and tried one thing after another en route to arriving at a unified styling approach. The virtual conferencing was a jarring departure from the traditional face-to-face exchange. But it worked.

7. Evolution

Pointilism
Braille inspired the pointillistic rendering of a whale on this leather coatdress. The textural rendering yielded tactility, allowed for touching and grasping the whale (Fig. 6). It was partly an exploration into the potential for experiencing apparel in the realm of touch (⟶ p. 53).

Nishijin-ori meets Brewed Protein™ materials
This dress incorporates a combination of Brewed Protein fibers and Nishijin-ori, a silk brocade produced by weavers in northwest Kyoto. The Brewed Protein fibers yield the striking sheen on the blue rendering of ocean waves (Fig. 4, p. 132). Here is a new textile genre begat of a centuries-old tradition and state-of-the-art technology. The luster is almost luminescent, the transparency unlike anything achieved previously with either silk or synthetics (⟶ p. 59).

Type-1
Here is an evolved version of our Type-1 technology, which allows for compiling fabric without using needle or thread. This new manifestation of Type-1 has broadened the range of design options. Adjusting the width of this wool coat along the back produces the desired girth. Type-1 technology thus accommodates people of different sizes (Fig. 8). Adding further to that accommodation are the options of attaching sleeves and hems of different length and width (⟶ pp. 60–61).

fig. 7

Biosmocking

The black crosses amid the complex intermingling of curves in these square and rectangular patterns indicate the openings for the neck. Inserting slits in a cross and submerging the fabric in warm water induces shrinkage suggestive of an umbrella closing. The slitted cross swells gradually upwards, and the surrounding portions of the fabric contract downward.

Creating apparel is ordinarily a matter of combining a front bodice and a back bodice to envelope the body. Biosmocking is a completely new approach that spawns a three-dimensional bodice without trimming away any fabric. It yields bodices of contours as complex as those seen here. The data for the contours resides in the digital domain, where it is available to adapt easily to any individual's physique and taste.

We assembled each dress for my Paris Haute Couture Week debut in 2016 from pieces of fabric shaped by hand, origami-like. With the Evoke collection, we used Biosmocking to derive garments—even ones of complex configuration—from single sheets of fabric (⇒ p. 65).

8. A Runway Show

Covid-19 would again preclude live shows and oblige us to remain online with our Evoke offerings for the fall/winter collection. I was determined, however, to restore the simplicity of models walking on the runway. We filmed the show at Osanbashi Hall, a spacious, 2,000-square-meter venue in Yokohama. The video is a straightforward recording of what unfolded there through careful choreography and lighting.

Digital processing engenders a freedom in video imaging that is appealing, but I wanted to recreate the excitement and creative tension of a live runway show. We therefore strived in our video presentation to impart the sense of viewing a fashion show in person.

Our models simply donned the apparel and strode the runway, though we had them reinforce the impact of the fashions with their gaits and facial expressions. We dimmed the lighting early in the show when the models appeared one by one, but we opened a curtain behind the stage to admit natural light for the show's latter half. The effect was one of emerging from a time of darkness into an era of hope.

Whales live between the ocean depths and the surface of the sea. They thus symbolize for me the dichotomy of the world of darkness and of light.

We scheduled the opening of the curtain for late afternoon. The weather forecast called for rain up to around the starting time for the show, so we resigned ourselves to having cloudy weather, at best, for the curtain opening. But as things unfolded, the rain lifted, and opening the curtain revealed a glorious sunset. Shadows in the vast hall mingled with the bright elements of the sky outside in a dramatic natural spectacle. Ryuichi Sakamoto's musical finale incorporated whale songs, bringing the show to a close with a powerful fusion of sound and light (⇒ pp. 72–112).

fig. 8

P. 5　EVOKE collection, Look 06

P. 7　EVOKE collection, Look 11

P. 17　フィッテイング風景（スタジオにて）

PP. 18-19　Voyager Golden Record より
ディスク（右上）と所収イメージ

P. 21　デザイン画の制作風景（スタジオにて）

P. 29　上：音の振動で声を可視化する実験
下：声のデジタルデータを
Biosmockingに応用する実験

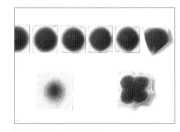

PP. 30-31　布片を使った
声の可視化のための実験

PP. 38-39　布片を使ったドレスのための実験

P. 40　布片を使ったドレスのための実験
P. 41　EVOKE collection, Look 05

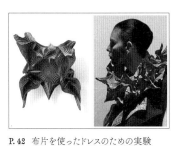

P. 42　布片を使ったドレスのための実験
P. 43　EVOKE collection, Biosmocking Neck

P. 9　EVOKE collection, Look 17

P. 11　EVOKE collection, Look 22

P. 13　EVOKE collection, Look 19

P. 22　基本イメージ
P. 23　クジラをモチーフにしたデザイン画

P. 24　上：Biosmockingのグラフィックデータ兼
　　　　設計図の制作
　　　　下：データを布に印刷
P. 25　印刷した生地を70度の熱湯に1分浸す

P. 26　水分を含んだ生地を乾燥・成形する作業
P. 27　EVOKE collection, Look 17

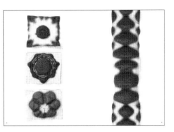

PP. 32−33　布片を使った
　　　　　　声の可視化のための実験

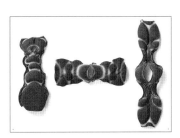

PP. 34−35　布片を使った
　　　　　　声の可視化のための実験

P. 36　EVOKE collection, Biosmocking Hat
P. 37　EVOKE collection, Look 19

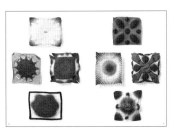

PP. 44−45　布片を使ったドレスのための実験

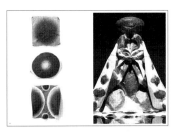

P. 46　布片を使ったドレスのための実験
P. 47　EVOKE collection, Look 27

PP. 48−49　Biosmockingの条件検証
　　　　　　（色の濃淡による縮率の違い）

P. 50　ランウェイショーの舞台裏で

P. 52　EVOKE collection, Look 01
P. 53　ドットグラフィックの試験

P. 54　EVOKE collection, Look 26
P. 55　パーツを組み合わせることで、
　　　部分的な劣化や体型変化に対応できる
　　　TYPE-1のシステム

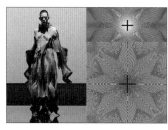

P. 62　EVOKE collection, Look 18
P. 63　Look 18のBiosmocking用グラフィックデータ

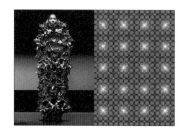

P. 64　EVOKE collection, Look 11
P. 65　Look 11のBiosmocking用グラフィックデー

PP. 72–73　ショー前日、会場にて
　　　　　（大さん橋ホール、横浜）

PP. 74–75　リハーサル風景

PP. 76–77　リハーサル風景

PP. 84–85　ショー直前の準備

PP. 86–87　ショーの幕開け

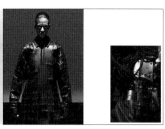

P. 56 EVOKE collection, Look 10
P. 57 パーツを組み合わせることで、
　　　部分的な劣化や体型変化に対応できる
　　　TYPE-1のシステム

P. 58 EVOKE collection, Look 07
P. 59 Brewd Protein™糸を使った西陣織

P. 60 EVOKE collection, Look 08
P. 61 デザイン画

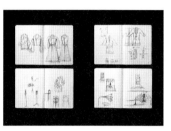

PP. 66-67 アイディアをかきとめたノート

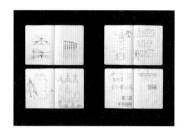

PP. 68-69 アイディアをかきとめたノート

PP. 70-71 アイディアをかきとめたノート

PP. 78-79 リハーサル風景

PP. 80-81 リハーサル風景

PP. 82-83 ショー当日の会場
　　　　　（大さん橋ホール、横浜）

P. 88 EVOKE collection, Look 01
P. 89 EVOKE collection, Look 01

P. 90 EVOKE collection, Look 02
P. 91 EVOKE collection, Look 03

P. 92 EVOKE collection, Look 23
P. 93 EVOKE collection, Look 15

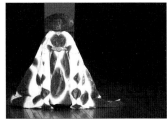

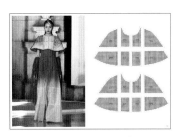

P. 100　EVOKE collection, Look 12
P. 101　EVOKE collection, Look 11

P. 102　EVOKE collection, Look 18
P. 103　EVOKE collection, Look 25

PP. 108−109　ショーのエンディングより

PP. 110−111　ショーのエンディングより

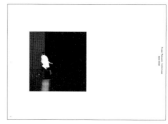

PP. 112−113　ショーのエンディングより

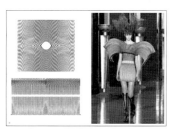

P. 120　Look 19のBiosmocking用
　　　　グラフィックデータ
P. 121　COSMOS collection, Look 19

P. 122　COSMOS collection, Look 17
P. 123　COSMOS collection, Look 13

P. 128　ATLAS collection Look 08

Photo Credits

Yasunari Kikuma: pp. 5, 7, 9, 13, 27, 36, 37, 41, 43, 47, 52, 54, 56, 58, 60, 62, 64, 124, 125, 128
Yuichi Ihara: pp. 50, 55, 57, 75, 76, 78−81, 84−87, 110−112
Shoji Fujii: pp. 82−83, 88−109, 114−116, 118, 119, 121−123
YUIMA NAKAZATO: pp. 17, 21−26, 29−35, 38−40, 42, 44−46, 48−49, 53, 59, 61, 63, 65, 66−73, 117, 120, 126−127

All works © YUIMA NAKAZATO

YUIMA NAKAZATO

Behind the Design

2022年5月10日　初版第一刷発行

企画・監修　学校法人 日本教育財団
企画協力　YUIMA NAKAZATO

翻訳　ミラー和空

発行人　藤元由記子
発行所　株式会社ブックエンド
〒101-0021 東京都千代田区外神田6-11-14 アーツ千代田3331
Tel. 03-6806-0458　Fax. 03-6806-0459
http://www.bookend.co.jp

ブックデザイン　吉野 愛
印刷製本　NISSHA

BOOKEND